MOVI

Jenny King was born in London in September 1940 – during the Blitz. She went to Godolphin and Latymer School in Hammersmith and then to Newnham College, Cambridge where she took a degree in English. After a PGCE teaching qualification at Nottingham, she taught in Shrewsbury for three years and then married and moved to Sheffield where she continued to teach. After taking early retirement, she did an MA in Contemporary Poetry at Sheffield University. She is the author of three pamphlets, *Letting the Dark Through* (1981), *Tenants* (2014) and *Midsummer* (2020).

JENNY KING

Moving Day

collected poems

CARCANET

First published in Great Britain in 2021 by
Carcanet
Alliance House, 30 Cross Street
Manchester, M2 7AQ
www.carcanet.co.uk

A CIP catalogue record for this book is
available from the British Library.

ISBN 978 1 80017 102 2

Book design by Andrew Latimer
Printed in Great Britain by SRP Ltd, Exeter, Devon

The publisher acknowledges financial
assistance from Arts Council England.

CONTENTS

for Edmund, and for Michael and Yvonne,
Frances and Tim, Freddie and Lily

MOVING DAY
Collected Poems

WALKING THROUGH SLACK

The village street tips me out into hills.
I watch the clouds canter on slopes far off,
on crests of the grassy mountains.
The midday peace is warm and edible.

Slackening pace at the lane's top, I see
the circle of the world.
Wonderful, the great presences of land
the sun is making play with

and wonderful in the mind how thoughts that lay
like stones in a dark landscape
moving at last
prepare themselves for speech.

ROCKERY

My neighbour's telling me what I could grow there
but my mind is unrolling the word
and here attached to the end of it is 'stones',
and at once I'm five,
playing in the garden with toy animals,
setting them up in hollows of damp gravel
between limestone peaks.
So many ages they've stood forgotten –
'You'll find plenty of things to plant there,' he says.

Behind the camels and elephants, in a wartime window,
a baby sucks at my mother's breast.
Yesterday I was allowed to watch
but today the twins are sickly
and I'm out here among sharp-edged rockery stones,
seeking company.
War comes from outside
but not their illness. My jealousy caused that.

Days later it's dark.
I'm in the armchair trying to cuddle
the fierce blue rabbit. The twins have died.
Guilty, I clutch its unloved head
and stare through no longer blacked-out windows
past the humps of the rockery
where the malevolent crocodile and tiger
crouching neglected
await their resurrection decades later
when a bewildered neighbour in another garden
suggests aubretia but is thanked with tears.

MILK

War's end:
we were resuming, in a shadowy world,
the burden of peace;
patiently, patiently beginning.
Outside the infants' dining hall
two air-raid shelter humps
(haunted, they said)
resembled graves.

Milk, white among dampness,
waited for playtime.
Job's Dairy, the bottle told me:
a patriarch, unseen in early morning,
clattering to school with rough crates
tangling his windy beard.

Then a first ha'porth of learning took hold of me:
it was job, like a job,
like something simple you get up and do.
War finished, you begin on peace
like a favourite pudding.

Later I was told, no, it was Jōb.
Peace harsh on the tongue,
chewy and difficult,
was cold and necessary like milk.
Single planes overhead at night
droned like speeches; through lanes at evening
went canvassers foraging for votes.

Milk, day by day appearing,
washed into us by ounces knowledge
of the new world and its ways.
At our next school
quiet men from big new dairies
made the deliveries, anxious about their rent.

EGG

Once upon a time on the bedroom mantelpiece –
a pimpled sandy brown, big as my head.
Surely out of a story, it could have been laid
by a phoenix in some fantastical tale
of Sinbad the Sailor

or by the last dodo, improbable bird.
Dodo? They told me how the crew sailed off
after unknowingly eating the last one.
No regrets for the taste of its foul, oily flesh.
Home, from the only island where it lived.

So was it the same for ostriches?
No, no! they told me,
ostriches flourish still and grow great feathers
women once wore to decorate their hats.
When was that? In dodo time?

CINEMA

When my mother was young
a boy would cycle up and run in breathless
from pedalling like the wind over Richmond Bridge
with Reel Two of *The Perils of Pauline.*

Now, eyes dazzled from *Fantasia,*
I hold her hand down the same stone steps.
Through the new dark where light had always lain,
a sleepy ride on the bus and the short walk home.
Then the best, the most wonderful thing –
looking up from a pavement made strange by night
to see overhead
stars, giving their miraculous show.

STAG BEETLE

My only sighting:
myself, aged seven,
pointing and crouching and chattering with the others:
the huge beetle, shiny as coal,
his great forceps borne like a battle-axe.
Heraldic, medieval creature
lost on the dusty pavement.

Going home from school was never more exciting.
The boy who boasted he'd put him in a matchbox,
the girl reaching to nearly touch those pincers,
the lookers-on poised for flight,
we stared, filled with amazement, part voyeur, part hunter,
while the quarry slipped away under a hedge
into the list of endangered species,
the children dispersing into middle age.

LETTING THE DARK THROUGH

Twinkling's a kind of shining
darkness irradiates,
not that brightness
we see in winter shops, nor sleepy glow
homegoing buses warm us with,
nor the white, solemn points of sun on sea.

Continuous yet broken,
as a tree masses leaves, distinct yet merged into one,
as a shingle beach is stones, that is, each stone,
so twinkling is bright but patched, the patches being
part of the light's quality.

Learning imperfection is a life's task,
the heroism of middle age
letting the dark through.

BORDERLAND

Beyond our boundaries, everything's in order,
bus stops neat, litter bins empty, each house
square to the road, its complement
of people sane and productive.

When the clocks change over there,
everyone puts down spanner or gardening fork,
picks up *Treasures of Literature* and says,
'Ah well! another year!' and is content.

Here we never catch up. Our calendars,
dishevelled leaves, keep shuffling
our missed appointments. Newspapers
lie piled on the fridge unread. Weeds grow in the dark.
Looking out at dawn, we watch mist riding the solid hills.

MIDSUMMER

At the stair corner where it turns for the attic
a shaft of sunlight strikes the step – only in June
for a moment at ten o'clock, just where sometimes
the moon looks in *en passant*
on its way to outer darkness –
like neighbours who call by once in a while
to ask if we'd like a bag of runner beans,
tell news of their travelling son and ask after ours.

The swifts swooping under the eaves to a hidden nest
keep this a family house. From a top window
I watch the infant rowan berries bob in the breeze
and I sit for a moment on the attic stairs
to consider this year in its fulness
before it slips away, one step at a time.

STARLINGS

Two shiny starlings sit on the chimney
conversing in whistles under a yellow-grey sky.
They have flown from a wintry place
and are discussing strategy. Listen! Under their breath
they are making plans for the gutter above that special spot
where the rotted end of a board leaves a front door.

We ask, *This is about to be spring then?*
No good asking the sparrows, who hide their nests in the hedge,
nor the blackbird who favours the heart of the Portuguese laurel,
still less the robin who sings on and on in our garden
but nests next door. None of these
will show you their private business.

Our starlings, though, keep flying up and down
to whichever is minding the eggs in their makeshift nest –
not secret, not romantic or beautifully formed –
flagged up by its trails of straw on the pebble-dashed wall.
Then there'll be nestlings. From upstairs we shall hear them,
like a classful of children chattering their way through spring.

TENANTS

The bees have found themselves a door
in the cracked pebbledash.
We watch, uncertain, while they make our home
theirs, and their storehouse too.

Now they keep busy in the clover flowers,
single minded, unshowy – householders
gathering in their harvest, more sure than us
and unafraid of winter.

VISITORS

When visitors come
openly up the path and ring the bell,
the door is set wide,
the house thrown open.

But garden visitors come by a hundred byways,
via bush, via eaves after long inspection;
the rook hauled down by his eye-strings
like a great shining kite tumbled on to the grass,
hedgehog by the leaf route in darkness,
woodmice by their street only the cat marks.

To the front door come
foreseen decisions, rational planning,
matters of season or the years -

as at a burial,
while the coffin's borne in with stately grief,
at the churchyard's neglected end stands
a man apart, hat under his arm, watching
a well-trained dog sniff under wreaths, behind vases,
loping out of sight, seeking the next death:

so over the hedge
trouble, anxiety, illness sail in on the wind
like the debris of autumn, dreamt of, unassailable.

ASLANT

Low sun scatters yellow across the garden
in handfuls, in between the shadows
where delicate trees portion it into threads.
So evening comes

aslant like someone slipping through a door
that's closing softly –
perhaps the end of something, or a chance
to think about it later.

Then darkness, like a choice you find was made
before you were aware, thickens
already in the corners. All the garden,
night coloured, speckled with white flowers, adrift.

NIGHT WATCH

In the dark, how steadily
four lamps return their gathered light.
Closer related to their parent sun
than to us who planted them, they give
the unseen garden their own geometry.

We think them ours, but if they had faces
they would turn them skywards, if they had legs
would march up and down together, out there
under the stars that spin so slowly across the black
till light pollution swallows them

the way dawn supplants these sentries, the way
our cat leaves his nightly patrols and sleeps
after long life. At the other end of the garden
we stir with daylight, while the lamps
return to foot-high sticks.

FEEDING THE SNAILS

Today when the woodpigeon never came
and blackbirds were inattentive, a damp dusk
falls on the little clumps of seed
scattered on garden paving.
Later, coming home under stars now,
I pass the uninvited at their feast,
small humps drawn close together,
helmeted night-time fancies.

My day of rational projects
melts into memory as half-ideas
slip in unasked under cover of darkness.
Indoors, I look out at unreadable trees,
revisit plans I made which break and drift
while clouds near the horizon
take their moonlit edges underground.

A SHORT SEASON

Blue sky slatted with cloud,
soft rushes of wind promising gales,
and the brown leaves beginning to crowd the bus stop –
summer was a short season.

Then light grew tall, flattening idle grass,
roses opened drily, and at night
radio music from cars' wound-down windows
blazed at the junction.

Now come the last appearances.
Rouletting past the loft window
the swifts take their final bow.
Sudden and soft under the apple tree
a marigold holds up its pretend sun
and shrinks and blanches.
The coat-cupboard loses the salt of rolled-up mats.
Out in the yard the leaf-fire ghosts are gathering.

A sense of turning,
patter of leaves between the ears,
rumouring change.
Last light behind the eyes. Ash in the mouth.

DAMSON TIME

Last week in Russell's fruit shop, suddenly
turning I called out *Damsons! I must have some!*
We were about to pay. I grabbed a handful,
he checked the weight – gave an inviting look,
dropped more, a few at a time, invitingly into the bag.

It was the week that buffers holiday time
from the start of autumn. 'Back end' they call it here,
people returning home but schools not in.

Later the smell of boiling jam
filled the kitchen with a harvest sweetness
like gathered summer. Then the filled jars
shone with a crimson tending towards darkness.

Soon pounds of blackberry would crowd the cupboard –
picked out of hedgerows off untamed brambles
whose inescapable thorns catch at the sleeve
will bring autumn's shadow into our kitchen.

We remember the signs –
curtains drawn early, bonfire smoke in the air,
winter clothes pulled from the wardrobe's depths.
The year swings to its equinox.
Days hurry from morning to night.

OUT IN THE BAY

We walked right out
over tide pools, squelching hummocks
and sharp rock ledges, to run alone
on the edge of the sand and to shout.

Running and shouting in and out
of runnels of escaping water, up and down
on the ribbed sand,
far far from the dry beach-foot
on the outermost pretence of land.

And we returned empty-handed.
Only echoes and footprints lingered
briefly between the pools.

Now, walking through the night that's newly arrived –
above the country road a matt, bright sky
and great trees embroidered with darkness –
I look on our dancing as a festival.

As the sandy moon shines
with its halved shape peculiar to this night
on a hillside slightly changed from week to week,
I remember our time of running in the empty bay.
Now sea covers where
your shouts and dances sang the song of today.

DASH

See the lime tree's eagerness –
halfway up the trunk's thin ridges
leaves burst through, before the busy sap
can power them to the top.
So children dash ahead, not knowing where
nor caring, till they wait at kerbs for the others.

Slowly the others follow,
watching their children out of reach
run dangerously fast, far in the lead
always, incautious tribe
happiest in motion.

Later, full grown, aware,
they'll keep the others company in a slow walk,
then leave and go far off,
spending their lives
with new companions and becoming
others, slowing in turn towards their autumn.

WAKING

Dark has gone away, the child said,
back to his nest. I remember
how he stood in his cot, cheerful as morning.

Nowadays dark lingers, hovers above,
waiting for the bad moments, the bad dawns
when daylight is not enough, when God
is in his heaven with the door closed.

Some mornings I wake afraid,
unable to prise off the claws of dark.
But today the blue gathers
above November's drift of leaves.

Innocent cirrus clouds
make off before a sharp wind.
I get up, move about, drink tea, talk,
leave the dark in his nest.

THE DREAM

Late at night:
the cat is studying shadows in the garden,
trees are sibilant in the wind.
Light rain ripples the window.

In the still house
I glance at the children on my way to bed.
Counting them, you call it: one, both.

He sleeps tangled in blankets, the bed a workshop.
She lies tidy as heroes. I look again
and her eyes half open, smiling. She told me once
she doesn't sleep at night but only dreams.

I pause by the bed. She glances, sleeps. Her dream
touches me like a long-cane, feeling, passing.
Though, a white witch,
she turns me into what she pleases,
yet her dream shows her no further into me
than my thoughts probe her life.
My waking digs no deeper – lightly we bob together.

I turn away, towards my own sleep.

IN THE WINDOW

I sit at the table, waiting.
The child eats slowly, stares about,
tide-wracked with me on the teatime shore.

Beyond her through uncurtained windows
darkness is thickly varnishing the garden,
till suddenly a brightness
stripes it with reflected light and shows
behind me the house lit and wakening.

Now in the dazzle-frame of doorway
laid like a mirage on the garden
(or, in the unreal holograph garden
where the electric fact shines) hopping comes
the image of a boy.

Hop, hop in the doorway,
in the doorway in the garden,
hopping reflected into room and garden –

by arriving, leaving along the sepia lawn;
coming, therefore going away
so lightly, so unaware.

SWIMSUIT

My daughter and I, upstairs in children's wear,
were hunting through holiday clothes –
at least, I was. She had wandered away.
Then suddenly she was there at my elbow
with a cherry-red swimsuit: 'Age 5,'
which she was. *Can I have this?* she asked.

I had assumed my choices were the best
but the next week, warmed by Italian sun,
I realised at length how she grew up
when in her cherry-red, with confident smile
she swam from me across the hotel pool,
that short but decisive distance
between my sunbed and the other side.

POINT OF BALANCE

I'm standing in the hall.
To my left, a commentator is amazed
about a long putt birdied at the twelfth.
Someone is coming down the stairs, declaring
United are ahead; behind me
a plaintive voice asks why this lampshade wobbles.

I'm trying to discuss when tea should happen.
The cat sulks past, upset by a strange toy
bought to amuse him. I get vague replies.
The phone rings; urgent feet thump to an answer.
My aged washing machine rocks into spin;
the T.V. peppers no one with applause.

The lampshade voice is gauging shades of blue;
the cat, consoled, slicks down his marmalade;
September yellows softly in; our world
must turn some more before the dark.
My focus switches, balancing, attention
pulled thinly sideways as the moments pass.

IN THE HOUSE

Because thoughts
because thoughts are not yet
       staggering against the door frame
because they are not yet ionized
but bristle in all directions
       cornering uncertainly – sleep does this
       rain on the loo window. Monday.
So to be is not necessarily
to contemplate being or indeed
       soap in its film of mud from weekend gardening
perhaps more visibly when nothing
consecutive interrupts but only
       clothes back to front both ways round
prickles of awareness. Very soon the day
is a shop blind pulled out,
a pattern of stripes emerging like purposes.

Stand in the hall, where doors like ears
stand open listening every way.
Stairs like bent knees walk up and down;
the telephone has its word to say.

Last year's framed photograph confronts
a fluttering calendar. The clock sleeps.
The stairwell skylight broods the house,
a mothering eye that shines and weeps.

Out from the kitchen beckon smells
of meals to come; the future's there
as steam, invisible but real.
Walk in and take tomorrow's chair.

Kitchen, where we settle
without obligation, comfortable among
sink, cooker, friendly domestic machines.
A world to our own scale; window-seat place
from where, drawn into the night like steam,
heat of an argument thinning, dispersing,
we watch the moon that watches us in turn,
rolling its white celestial eyeball
in a socket of space.

From the indoors out, our grounded existence
contemplates those enormous journeys.
I sit and remember
what you told me, that unhappy week.

Seen from space, our globe is small and hard
as a new potato.
Last night I walked pavements beside a valley,
wishing away some facts,
and the moon rose, very large,
clearing tree tops in a slow bounce.
It was the colour of red earth and veined
with unexpected richness;

so big and honeyed it seemed nearer
than the usual pale platter.
I would have liked to stroke it
and lap its texture round my desert thoughts.

We only looked at each other. 'You down there,'
said the moon, 'far off and seamed with mortality,
are you solid and rough to the touch, or is it only
fingers of light shaping confused distance?'

Here, hold this potato in your hand, I said,
small, solid, with its red, Egyptian dust.
Folk wisdom of the kitchen. You laid it by
and went to phone.
I took a damp cloth, wiping away fragments
to leave mud lines like rivers on the moon.

AT THE PUMP

Filling my car
I glance up from the pump and find I'm standing
where I once played in the dusk of chestnut trees
till bats flicked the switch of the dark
and looped out across the rusting steel
of a country railway line
that is concrete now.

I'm facing a raw new building, institutional brick.
The pump flips off, tank full. I hold my purse,
half turned towards today, and trip
on hidden wires of time and place, vanished
yet present in my head; an unexpected tug.
I pause, and the trap of memory clicks shut.

Once, travelling north in Canada
with my teacher-aunt to visit the wilderness school
where she'd begun, as long ago again
before the time of my playing here,
we passed the silent lake
and found her square log building filled with barley,
crammed to the roof, and all the people gone,
the exchange of voices dried to a treasury.
I think of her wondering survey and how we drove
back to the city banqueted on silence.

FAMILY HISTORY

A pond, described, shines in my memory.
My father cycles past – I don't know why
nor where it was. Too late to ask.
But there was a pond.

He said *his* father told of signing on
for the Boer War: 'Walk round the block and come back older.'
Checked, the war's dates and his don't quite accord
but for evidence we've his photographic plates.

Of my great-grandfather, only the census sheets,
a Square on the A to Z, the names of brothers
living – no listing then of infants dead.
So we can go

by bus through unknown streets, puzzle
at houses nothing like they were. We're left only
scatters of anecdote and some earthenware;
bones without flesh,

only the 'Who-on-earth?' at a tiny face
among posed lines of stares in their sepia best.
Just the census-taker's findings and the registrar's
patient quill

sliding away as the years pass, further still
from a look and a voice and even the half-knowledge
that is sure of a real pond somewhere,
a glimmering place.

The album shows you in black with a big hat.
My father tells me how you took him to France,
crossing the Channel on a ship with sails.

Whether in youth you ran about in the sun
or danced or played the piano I don't know.

I was told you lived in a big house in Lewisham,
lost sons in two wars. That your children called you
Mater. That you were widowed.

What you did between breakfast and bedtime
or who you spent your days with, I have no one to ask.

I remember, as a small child they took me to see you.
You sat, hands in your lap. We stared at each other,
two pairs of unfathoming eyes.

What you were hoping, or whether, as it appeared,
you felt your great-grandchild wasn't a patch on the dead,
I have no idea.

HINGED MIRROR

It begins with a voyage,
a sea-going great-great uncle. Adventurer? Merchant?
He comes home carrying gifts – oriental,
with all the meaning the plumed phrase implies.

The triptych mirror stands on three small feet.
On the back a fine, long-whiskered gentleman
parades with his banner, a servant
carries his shield, its terrible pointed boss.

Fold it up: on the front a dragon,
fierce open jaws, a scaly ring of body,
the backing, a thin sheet of ivory.
The mirror settled in my grandmother's house.

Now four generations have infused the glass
with leisurely or urgent looks. It breathes them back
and sends a kind of warmth across our room
like seas that have absorbed the summer sun.

1912

Sunlight. The shadows of twelve dangling feet,
laced boots at different heights, patch the brick wall
where someone set these children in a row
in their smocked dresses, coatless in the warm.

Dorothy on the left, hair short and neat.
Tall Hilda's, on her left, flows dark and free.
Then Fred aged six, the only boy, in shorts,
then Winnie with her bucket on her knee.

Next, not a sister, sits with hands behind,
balanced uneasily beside her friend
Kathleen, who has invited her along
and leans near, settled kindly on the end.

A freeze-frame from our history, moment of stillness
before two wars. My 'Scarborough aunts' and here,
the only surviving boy, my father-in-law.
The thread pulls tight – I twitch the end and stare.

Thirty years later three of them returned.
Dorothy, long since widowed, cooked for them all.
Hilda saw to the church on Castle Hill.
Winnie phoned, visited – always tales to tell.

I tuck their picture under a folder's edge,
their six heads sticking out. They gaze at me.
Though I deprive them of their hands and feet,
yet still they speak and see.

THE LEAF CLEARER

The head of an old broom inspired my grandfather,
as if Leonardo stared at a wheel and invented cycling.

Next-door's broken mower supplied a frame. Now
he looked for what others had overlooked –

cans for an axle to stick bristles on,
handle from a wrecked pushchair in the hedge.

A treasure hunter quartering a field and finding silver.
Quick, before the wind stole his prey of leaves!

Assembled, pushed, adjusted. An inward smile
like some Brunel seeing travellers cross his bridge,

or God in his deckchair on the seventh day.
Then off to use it, triumphant over junk-blind neighbours.

LEAVING TOWN

A dazzle, a white sheen
the snow throws against the black sky,
undoes the night;

just as my grandfather,
shrewd old man, laid newspapers down
to cast up light on his own face

for the photograph,
and leant forward into the reflected shine:
so now the hills do, as we

swoop down the empty road
and up again to the high, lonely roundabout
from which the evening city behind shows

like a tossed down cloth, roughly spread.
Though we travel together as naturally
as snow comes, yet the sudden hills observe us,

unmoored from their distance without warning,
like unexpected occasions;
familiar road, strange, bright hills, a life continuing.

GERMAN EXCHANGE

i.m. my father, George Greatwood

The future in the past:
I would like to have joined
those two men walking by a German lake,
ignoring age and deafness,
language teachers resolved to be understood,
trudging along.

Fifty years ripple by them in the dark water:
they remember their friendship.
Told of that afternoon, I flow back too
into postwar childhood. On the kitchen table
a letter from my father to his friend with the umlaut
waits to be posted.

The country is 'reconstructing'
and they're setting up an exchange between their schools.
Parties of boys collect on our station platform
eager for travel – beside loft-dusty luggage
trying out phrases of peace: *Danke schön. Guten Morgen.*
Auf Wiedersehen.

Along the shoreline path
side by side in a sharp wind
the teachers are walking across the decades,
laying them down, a delicate trapeze
above the death of wives, departure of children,
retirement, days of silence –

talking now English, now German, nodding agreement
until with a *ja* and a *ja* they arrive
at the present and pause, watching how water
in its invisible flowing through the black lake
makes for the sea, their thoughts jumping hopeful
into the future.

THE COPPICE

The birds are flying up from heathy ground,
out from under a dangling pine branch.

She flies ahead, he follows – airborne
in the imagined country of the past.
On the back, 'The Coppice'. Yes?
I doubt you coppice pine trees.

A painted dream of pre-war country living
without the guns. But why else pheasants?
No threatening wood – the detail's careful –
but landscape of English gentry.

Tired of 'Utility B' plain wartime china
my mother seizes on it.
On the back of every plate a lion on a crown
declares we're through, and safe.

And then we're through but find we're never safe.
Since that war's end seven decades see
the constant visitation of more wars,
threats, stand-offs, recessions, pandemic.

To what green country can we now return?
'Before the war.' *Which war?* The children ask.

A FOUNTAIN SEALED

Hurrying down the hill, the bicycle
(a hundred years ago) jolting her, little pebbles
of knowledge like the undigested dumplings
inside her, my mother

belts back to school for French conversation
at one o'clock. The aunt has insisted,
as usual, on a Proper Lunch.
There is no time.

Language runs in her head and like water
splashes whatever she does with exact
lace-patterns of words, intertwined,
neatness and power.

The formal entrance (as she rattles in,
parks the bike, running,) insists, 'Knowledge
is now no more a fountain sealed.'
Droplets of something

fly from her hair; speech is a sapling,
a diviner's rod. The spring flows over,
the steady streams of learning trickle in,
her tributaries.

Only the benefactor-aunt, encoded
in little rituals, refrains from speech.
Unsayable deep tides rise in silence,
burdened with dumplings.

MENDING

Like a camel struggling at the eye of a needle,
my mother at her preparations
to 'cobble up' a tear in my school dress.

Licking the thread to a point,
face screwed up, she kept trying
until at last with a *Got it!*
she pulled the recalcitrant end
out on the sunny side of the eye.

The mending, the post-war making do,
sides-to-middling of worn sheets,
her agony at knitting, all shook down into ease
as she sat up in bed on a Saturday night
listening to the radio play.

I lay beside her, allowed to stay up for a while
and watch her slide socks one at a time
on to the green plastic mushroom,
while with a darning needle she worked her way
through the navy, the brown, the charcoal –
confident now in her task, in her peaceful kingdom.

WILSONS

Some of the present-day Wilsons of Sheffield can trace
their ancestry back to the fourteenth-century Wilsons
who lived on the edge of the moors.
– David Hey

Go back. Not to the folk
braving December cold on the moor's edge,
'the sons of Will' scratching a hard living,
wives and children toiling from cottage to fold,

but to a hilly field on the outskirts of town.
Twentieth century. What was it doing there –
Henry Wilson's marble water trough
marooned on too-tall legs among the flock?

Where had it stood first? Maybe beside a road
now lost in the new townscape,
then pulled from a builder's skip.
Later, too unwieldy,

abandoned, clinging to existence in a field
like the first Wilsons. Names endure
as features do in faces down generations,
given, not chosen.

My neighbour bought it, lorry'd it home,
placed it among the daffodils near his house –
tribute (it says) from Henry's sons and daughters
in a garden which was once a moor.

KENSAL GREEN

Grieving or curious, people come to his counter
naming their recent or ancestral dead
set here beside a railway's sudden clatter.

Some pass by his office. A woman
with pushchair, navy mac and pink umbrella
takes the left-hand path which hugs the wall.

Indoors, he shows on a map the graves they seek,
pressing his index finger down:
'Here. Just about here.'

On the far side, the woman with the pushchair
passes children's graves at a steady speed
as though she knows the way.

Outdoors, some are distracted, pause to read –
William and Jane dead in 1860.
Tucked on the base, his age crumbled, Henry their son.

The woman with the pushchair halts by the wall,
takes violets from her bag and lays them down.
She didn't need his help.

He prints out fresh maps ready for more callers.
It starts to rain. Going back inside
he marks the site of next day's burial.

ASH

When Alice Clitheroe, aged ten, fell
out of her old life
head downwards,
three rooks were flying far above the tree,
two colts raced, manes in the air, across the meadow
and a squirrel watched in surprise from a high twig.

On the way down she parted with
school friends, favourite games,
bike, ambitions,
her reason for climbing that particular tree –
which they never discovered –
her history project, her riding lessons.

Reaching the ground
she entered the grassroots kingdom of chairs and lino,
sunlight in corridors, wheelchair-squeak on tiles,
motherly women with mops and disinfectant,
visitors bringing photos.
A seated, indoors world possessed her.

Sometimes she looks, wordless, through the window
where birds and clouds go by.
Rain pats the glass, then brown leaves.
She is Alice still:
this is her Saturday job, her backpacker's hostel,
degree course, employment, marriage; her life and her death.

SHEPHERD WHEEL

Below steep pavements warm in the sun
and lightness of the open valley,
below dry banks where roots protrude
and then curve back among leaf-litter,

right down by the scurrying stream
the grinding hull sits, stone shed
squatting by the water.
Dark inside as a ship's hold,
freighted with beams, troughs, shadows.

'By midwinter,' he says, 'you can't see
past three o'clock. Think how they sat,
there, facing the mean windows, the wheel going
and a candle as only help,
grinding their blades all day, a meagre living.'

Their darkness is in here still.
As evening comes it trickles insidiously
from dips, from corners like a cargo shifting
and the warden, tall captain, stands alone,
back to his glowing fire in the iron grate,
and hears the leaking pentrough splash outside,
a steady sea carrying his ghosts and him.

STAINED GLASS

Unchanged for centuries. Yet the saint's feet
darken as her halo thins, her motto pales.
Glass creeps, liquid, down into her toes.
She is becoming earthly again.

Her cloak still throws blood on the stone floor.
Could heaven abandon her after all this time?
She stares out as though ready to suffer her martyrdom anew.
Meanwhile she is claimed like us by gravity

which insists on weightiness.
Though defiant, her stance admits
that she is always sinking,
and sanctity is heavy work and never finished.

HOLLOW WAY

So to begin in the middle, as they all did,
picking up a journey anywhere,
packmen, higglers, carriers of all sorts
over moors, through woods
to any hamlet that would have them.

If you couldn't read, it was enough
to know T for Tideswell, C for Chesterfield
and a few more – traipsing through bog cotton,
its white fluff up to the pony's hocks.
Trudging over the wind-sharp ridges

then down past starveling hawthorns
following a track worn deep
like the floor of a burrow. Shelter of a sort
between earthbanks. An eerie loneliness
on misty days but grand in the heat.

At the end a barn, a house or two. Voices.
Bread and ale maybe, on lucky days; else
well-water from the palm of your hand.
A human sound – someone to talk to.
Make a sale? Good. A night in a barn? Better.

On then up over the tops to wherever-it-is,
but you won't be stopping.
Down again and the path
under the traffic of feet sinks a little
each year. Whins clutch at the bank.

REPORT TO THE VALLEY CAMP

We went to reconnoitre
up Fox Hill, looking out
for any file or scout,
high pass, wooded stream-crossing,
fortified place or any important feature.

So, Sir, we climbed the crags.
What we saw then amazed us. Clouds go by
like close companions. Swifts and merlins fly
bathed in those regions as their own.
But most of all, the distance! and the height!

What of strategic value?
But the moist clouds – as close as me to you!
It's bare up there, moorland. A rendez-vous
with the birds' landscape, with the sun and moon.
You're a king there, believe in power like flight.

Yes, Sir, strategic: no, we didn't see
marks of activity or groups of men
or anything suspicious. Now and then
we heard the lark, in acres of air. I think
this land is more important than we knew.
I saw no strongholds – but the view! the view!

THE MILL, CHATSWORTH

Set down from the road, outlier among green,
the old mill swallows light as rocks do.
We saw its wall as solid as the hill
under the bright frost.

Four deer came down the slope,
stags, at a gallop; flecked like the smooth river
which they sprang into, bounded through, and left
without pause.

We saw them leap on up the other side
into the stag-brown copse. The building,
still as earth, showed its bleak face to us.
Then we climbed

and suddenly from above saw it was roofless
and hollow as a tube, as when
an unexpected death presents a life
suddenly to be looked down.

At the bottom of this shell of walls
grass lay. We were seeing down the tunnel
of an old kaleidoscope, like the park itself.
The deer shake it with their galloping
and make beads on the continuous river beside it.

Take the main road from city to distant city.
Here's the world's business say Tesco, Plumbing Solutions,
Maersk, National Express and Royal Mail.
This, say the lorries, matters.
It's what keeps you going.

Off to the side, the village names suggest
a slower, older world. The sign says
Lobthorpe and Swayfield, sounding permanent,
like under-pinning,
earth and what belongs there.

Swayfield has land for two ploughs in Domesday Book.
Lobthorpe, 'the fugitive's hamlet', is smaller, poorer,
warrants just fifteen words, yet it's still there
at the end of lanes.
The two names tell us

Here is what you'd forgotten in your haste.
Leave the self-important road and go there.
Take the turn-off between quiet hedges
and find a pub
with usual football-talk.

The Great North Road chops through Hell Lane, passes
Wood Nook, then skirts a transport testing station –
beyond where Ermine Street,
like those who made it, has vanished
among fields.

CHISWICK STEPS

Look down from this paved path into dark water.
Behind you cyclists, joggers, scooting children
pass briskly in the sun. On the opposite shore
parakeets scream and squabble through trees.
At the river's edge, the heron, patient as reeds.

A shine of mud, then a few yards of causeway
below the draw dock where hauled-up barges
brought hops for breweries, took the island's osiers
while the slack river rested. Some days it rose
as it does still, to lick the feet of houses.

Now go below into a middle region
thick with flotsam:
modern rubbish – broken plastic, cartons,
and all the junk pushed by its current
into the foul embrace of the litter-trap.

At last, here's the bottom,
ground unvisited for a thousand years
where lost and fallen things remain,
rest and roll and rest again
abraded by the up and down of moving water.
Barge chains. Coins with forgotten kings.

STOREHOUSE

To catalogue everything
this back-street workshop hoards
would be a task for holy patience:
the sun that beats in at this door
would need to stand
quietly waiting as I do myself
till mysteries are complete.

Open-mouthed, a car
stands tilted up to show the engine.
Behind its gleaming white,
racks and stacks of dark and oily tools
blend into gloom
under the sooty skylight
by the iron wall.

Cupboards with closed doors powdered in chalk sums,
ledges of spanner ends like cotton reels,
magnetic strips
holding through pure love tens of screwdrivers
arranged by size.
A dish of drained oil, glimmering.
A box of drills.

It's because I'm free
to know nothing of all these purposes
that I can loiter at the open door
irresponsible as the breeze-blown leaf
which drifts in circles a moment
and choosing the sump-oil, sinks,
becomes one with the place,
leaching into its fabric
below the surface.

RUNNERS IN TOWN

Runners slip through the crowd, nip
round shopping-heavy pushchairs, on
past gossiping groups and are gone
into a sort of fourth dimension.

Hardly present, they slide
between minute and minute, intent
on escaping what time once meant,
while shoppers stare, asking each other

Was that Paul? Was that Sue? unsure
whether the flickering figures half seen
from behind might have been
the friends they knew, or thought they knew.

CHESIL BANK

A tick, a tack, a shushing
of numberless brown pebbles
amassing and assembling a dry hill.
Sparse thistles set out for the summit
but the slope slides under them, muttering
The shore is private.

It has bought up the seabed in lots
and is planning to auction it off
for a million front gardens.
It rejects the term *beach*
but welcomes the fierce undertow of tides.
Swimmers avoid its dragon clasp.

Shingle is its name,
a whole creature that forms and turns
unceasingly. Eighteen miles
before the shore is at peace, before donkeys and sandcastles
reclaim possession of their ice-cream world
from its growling stones.

SHORELINE

August. The long tide
creeps out at Walberswick.
Ripple upon ripple of water,
ripple upon ripple of wet sand.
Gulls plane over their own reflections.
Children investigate with inquiring toes
which find the ground uncertain,
a shifting mix of sea and land.

They trample gently, watching
small lace of foam ride to their ankles
then raise their eyes to distance.
Nothing but water – behind them, solid ground.
Between, the sort of compromise
their feet are first to learn.

SCAR

Sandy Suffolk dunes look down
where concrete blocks defend the beach.
Above in the heather
scraps of barbed wire, rusted to soil-brown,
conceal themselves until

running for the sea
I trip and catch a small sharp wound
(the landscape invaded still,
tricky with war rubbish, eight years into peace.)
The neat round blemish

lasts all this time
as memories do. Both shore and heathland
remember their history,
defences sunk out of sight, leaving behind
red-brown earth, white scar.

WAVES

I keep coming back to the to and fro of them,
rhythmic movement of the sea's edge.
A child, amazed by the endless slip and lift,
I watched to see how high it would come,
how far down it could retreat.

Shore breeze, gulls' cries, briny kelp smell,
the underfoot shifting of damp sand,
grew tangled into the waves' presence
where I stood staring or running forward and back,
involving myself in the elements.

These days I watch for the pauses. Like breath filling
and emptying, a moment of balance comes between in and out,
between out and in,
like someone saying, *Really? Let's think about that.*
For a moment the world is not changing but listening.

OCEAN

Ripples hand themselves over again and again
to the lap of the land,
curling up and across like conjurors' fingers
but today the woods invite me
and I turn my back on the sea. This
will be a forest day.

Far out, ideas rise up like hectoring rollers
and sweep shorewards.
The offing swells with ideas which sway,
collide and clash in foam.
The heaviness of water is too much to think of,
I struggle against it.

Woods with their individual thoughts,
twigs and leaves
held out like hands each in their perfect detail,
reach out to receive me
asking as I arrive
Could you settle for this?

Tomorrow when I have walked a while in the woods
I must go back,
paddle through ripples then swim out
past the moored boats
to dare big waves which rise and fall, converge and part
continuously.

SARDINIA

Moored Boats

That man and wife who kiss
out in the sea between the moored boats
are German, it appears.
Her black, Babylonian cap
describes her as a thriving dress-shop owner.
They swim about together.
Walking on sand, he shows a heavy figure:
she smiles at him, fair-haired on land,
and buoys him up.

Afternoon Wind

The wind of afternoon shivers the trees.
Think of it as a brown goat,
hot, small, distant,
picking its way over dry country.
Think of it as a fish,
slipping through clearness, crossing water
in swift glides.
Think of it in winter as a coach
rocking through mountains, black with rain.

CANAL COTTAGE

Low on the skyline, Birmingham's restless glow
but here the night is merely darkness

afloat on quiet, as though water was silence
that filled the cup of the lock to overflowing.

Between the shadowy reedbed and the towpath
it waits for daylight, for movement, people

passing upstream with a sorting out of levels,
with voices calling, the gentle rise of boats.

I lean into night from an upstairs window.
Trees on the opposite bank score a clear sky.

Already I hear the thrush
who sings all day. Glints of ripples appear.

Light comes. The lock is emptied, filled.
Freed water plunges on its way downhill.

TO THE ROUND POND

Do you remember how cold it was
in Kensington Gardens?
We skimmed ice fragments over the frozen pond –
rr-rr-rr they went, singing.

Sixth-formers out for a lunchtime spree,
we knew our futures in those days
and came rejoicing, poised on the end of winter,
primed for spring. You in your red scarf.

Mothers with wool-warm pushchairs hurried
past Peter Pan in his stillness.
We in our duffled youth ran laughing
down the long paths

that met and separated,
till now they meet again and we turn
surprised to see the pond such years behind,
ourselves so changed.

VOICE

Salt identifies itself in water
and once my brother in a science mood
said *Close your eyes — let's see
with how little salt you can still taste a difference*
and took a plain and a painted cup to the tap.

Blindfold, I heard him fill one, then salt and fill
the second and bring me that, but I knew already,
for as it filled, it had told me which it was —
the painted one. The white one had no voice.
I never knew before that china spoke.

I think of the old drinking fountain on Ham Common,
the chained iron chalice where I lipped like a horse
tasting its wintry cold in summer heat.
It rang like a bell when I filled and lifted it,
the sliding water making its own tune.

I look out of the window into a world
noisy with contraries. Far in the past
lie times when I tried to catch one note alone.
Now I hear deep and treble sounds together
like evening bells in some Italian dome.

GOAT

Old goat, two inches high,
carved from some dark wood in a Swiss valley
seventy years ago,
the painted bell on your neck still sounds
for your first owner and all the dead.

This morning as I lift you from beside my cow
I see your udder, plain as day.
How did I never notice in all these years?
Did I assume, because you were my brother's
who was older, stronger, that you were male?

Did I suppose that being male
gave him power beyond what I could hope for?
Fifteen years since he died.
Now I have passed his age. I hold his toy
as though an amulet against forgetting

and feel the decades flowing through my fingers
like water pouring down the cascade at Chatsworth
that makes its way patiently, out of sight,
then bursts from the heart of the lake
and moistens the air with its tall plume.

But looking from my window at the world
I think how sisters have biased opinions
and how I never understood that sometimes
memory's not a wisp of falling water
but a small, unexpected, solid thing.

Let's lay three objects in a row:
cushion, darkroom bulb and crimson jacket.

The cushion cover is bright orange crochet.
It knobbles on my cheek but keeps me safe,
asleep through air-raids under the dining-room table.

Next decade the red bulb in the attic shows
my brother at his photographs,
the tray of fixer where his life emerges,
reluctant private ghost. Below the hatch
I sit on the bed and read to him, Ginsberg's *Howl*.

In Italy later I wear the crimson jacket
on black canals and through dank underpasses.
Then in Florence new-born Venus sails,
woman already, driving her shell to land,
not looking back.

FRIEDLAND STATION

A green field. The last train from the east.
This is what I remember.
A surge of people as it neared,
passengers leaning out of every window.
The country halt.

We were mere lookers-on, the visiting English,
but the German crowd
carried us with them where the fear and hope
were flooding west with the train, while the wall was built
and Berlin split.

In a whirl of sound the train whisked in
and I remember
a tall man running, staring, seeing, calling
Friedrich! Friedrich! A passenger springs from a carriage
and runs towards him.

And they were all just in time. I also remember
thirty years later,
the radio on as I painted our bedroom ceiling,
while brick by brick the wall fell to the crowd
and time collapsed on itself.

Before the days of texting, here's my mother
leaning across the sink to tap the window
at my father, weeding.
She places one index finger across the other: 'Tea.'
Looking up, he waves,
turns to survey his work then parks the hoe.
She fills the pot, carries the tray through.

The nestling's gape, the ladybird's spotted badge
give meaning without words: the tulip offers
its stripey bugle; yellow flowers
primp the forsythia. Under the little bridge
small dappled fish declare themselves as gravel.
The lonely man hang-gliding over Stanage Edge
feels what the winds tell as they clear the ridge.

Now after so long, you and I
find ourselves humming tunes the other started
in a different room, or guessing thoughts
from a slight inflection, look or trick of the eye.
Invited to 'tweetle' when tea's ready, I 'Olly, olly!'
the old Cam racers' cry, to call my cox,
deep in twelfth-century rivalry, from his books.

THE WEDDING SEASON

As we drove south from Delhi,
garlanded lorries stood
loaded with massive speaker horns,
waiting like elephants
for something they remembered to begin.
Streamers were part of it, and little flags,
ponies in pink cockades and shiny bells,
and once a man in jeans
trotting bareback on a white horse
to go and meet a bridegroom.

A sort of rose-pink joy was in the air.
We had been told, each year just at that time,
a few days after *Diwali*, it was the same.
We gazed, knowing we'd be home in one more week
to celebrate half a century of marriage.

That prodigal outlay colouring each road
showed us our own first hopes, long-weathered,
a familiar feeling
even amid the foreignness of the place.

PHYSIC GARDEN

The grandchildren kept asking *When's Mummy coming?*
Soon, we told them. *Soon.*

Recovering from last month's emergency,
at last you had brief leave from hospital –
time off the ward to join us in those gardens.
So we sat waiting, that fine Saturday.

The children ran about on the maze of paths.
The sun shone and crowds gathered at the café.

Then suddenly, there you were
and all the flowers stood up a little higher.
Your children ran back, calling out to greet you
and you sat down with us, and said,

I'm hungry now! What shall we have to eat?
And the green herbs floated their good around you.

FIVE THOUSAND ACORNS

I remember you first as a teenager,
only child of my eldest aunt, the obliging cousin
down on all fours giving me rides on your back
round their sitting room carpet.

Met rarely as you grew up. Travelled for a vintner
later on, through French vineyards full of new-made friends.
You would move there, you said, in retirement –
which arrives, so we wait, without news.

But then, months later,
the promised phone call, and at last I know
you're in France, settled. Unsettled,
living alone in half a château.

I've been tidying the grounds, you say,
and I've picked up twenty bags of acorns.
Would you like some? – laughing,
for I'm in England, amazed at such a garden.

A foolish move, some thought – or brave and determined.
I imagine you – big, stiff-moving, an eighty-year old man
making that face I remember
that says *Job to be done.*

Then you're dead and I picture you with your rake,
beating the bounds of that lately bought domain,
gathering up, amazed, five thousand acorns.
The winds of Burgundy rattle them down.

MARGARET

I go to the cupboard, bring
the last crumbled scraps of thyme –
a world away from a Greek hillside, yet
I close my eyes and smell a hot, far-off place.

My afternoon is planned.
I shall go into town on a bus and pass
Thyme Café where, once Lockdown was over,
Margaret and I were to meet.

.

Stalled at the dried herbs
by thoughts of that unkept promise,
I turn my mind to the front,
to the future where all my actions

shall be straight lines without
the hiss and blur of interference,
stray memories nudging against my purposes
to push them sideways.

The bus smells of diesel and disinfectant,
of today and tomorrow. We sail past the café.
Margaret has died so this is not my stop.
I look ahead.

NORFOLK

Suddenly everything is bigger –
oak trees shadowing the road
have trunks a doorway wide,
stretches of wheat are plains,
rivers unsatisfied by channels
colonise the woodland into Broads.
Above the enormous beet fields, sky
is a blue ocean thronged with towers of cloud.
From each extreme horizon
a spire thrusts upward from a village.

Only the larks preserve their modest borders,
share out the sky in boxes.
Only the lanes, no wider than called for,
ease hedges into nooks for cars and tractors.

RANMOOR

Stately as women at a funeral
but bridal white
the clouds go by. They've seen it all before.
They pass indifferent to the earth, its noise
from trivial business on the valley floor.

How high and how unreachable they go,
minute by minute
sailing along the seaways of the sky,
their own unhindered pace not fast, not slow,
letting the troubled landscape trickle by,

while we down here trapped in the jam of days
look up sometimes in envy
imagining ourselves as high, as free
to form, fragment or lose our shape in haze
or drift across the wide impersonal sea.

CLOUDS

Two clouds like mother and child
hurry across the blue of the attic window.
Tall, thin, they lean eagerly into the wind
and when I look again, have gone.

Vanishing trick of the sky.
Forms that won't wait, larger and smaller
scurrying off behind the edge of the pane
which holds all we see.
More follow, torn and twisting, blowing after
the mother cloud. They'll never catch her.

DEPARTURE

Sitting in the top-floor study
I look out at clouds and think
I could open this window and step through.
I kneel on the desk, free the latch and clamber
into the sky, one hand on the tiles to steady me.
The breeze that suddenly pulls me free is warm.

Now I am cycling the air, legs and arms
working as though in water as I find my way
bit by bit over the tall trees opposite.
Seeing the floodlights of United's ground
I set a course, buffeted by soft gusts,
and meet a crowd of airborne travellers.

Nice day! a woman calls as we sweep down
and settle on the station roof like pigeons.
Daddy, why are we here? a child asks.
He tells her quietly, *This is the terminus.*
Now all at once I see – we are the dead
waiting in this warm spot for heaven to open.

A stir begins. We start to look about
and see below on Platform One somebody
holding a whistle. *Here we go! At last!*
the cry goes up. *Look there!* The clouds are parting
clear over Sheffield station and a tall angel
in boots and golden tunic waves us through.

THE COWS

In the middle of the night the cows came
breathing their hay-breath into the silent kitchen
and I, turning in my cold bed above,

was also there among them – felt their motherly warmth,
saw their shadowed flanks, gleam of damp muzzles,
sensed the flick of their tails across the cupboards.

Companionable silence. So I slept,
woke with the light, looked out and saw the herd
leaving in a slow walk over the meadow.

ABOVE THE STREAM

Sleeping in the converted mill with water
slipping by underneath to where the one swan
kept his place in the current with invisible strokes
through the anywhere of darkness

till the marshy horizon brightened,
even before waking we half recognised
the soft bustle of cows below the window
footing our sleep like rain.

We rose above the cool stream to a daylight
of eating, talking, exploring.
Drawn back at night to sleep out
the gap till morning's rational circumstance,

we lay leaning our ears to water's insistence,
hearing our memories and dreams
flow out where cattle grazed
and wind among slow saltings to the sea.

MAN WITH A DOG

Step out of bed – sunlight is halving
the unfamiliar valley, light from deep shadow,
the dark slope full of trees. A sandy track
leads up to sun on meadows.
A man with a dog has stopped to watch
two others coax a yellow machine uphill.
I hear its engine coughing as they heave
and pause and heave, until

I am half here and half there.
Just so, a child in the top of the bus,
I would stare at one familiar mansion,
its perfect lawn, sash windows. Inside,
figures half seen, people I longed to be
simply because of difference, sure
their selves beyond the glass more real than me.

And now, though I long to walk that opposite slope
beside the man with the dog, I turn to the room,
step back from other lives into my own.

One moment makes the difference
between the thoughts of a man running,
running for the bus, reaching the corner,
and the next second – the explosion bursting
windows, hurling shards of glass
into the brickwork where, slowed by his good breakfast,
nearly round the angle of the shopfront, he springs back,
turns with his arm over his face from the dusty blast
and retreats, safe.

Between the before and after,
an indivisible moment holds
an idea that breeds a discovery,
the child's sudden grasp of otherness
or the 'fiat' that begins the whole messy process of living.
Or the empty microsecond when, missing a step,
you tumble down to land surprised
full length at the foot of the stairs.

The man draws back, horrified.
Something has happened,
sharp and unchangeable,
intersecting here with now, making the moment before
a different age.
He hesitates, looks round, wonders
what's to be done.

INCIDENTAL

What he's after is a Noah's Ark
so nearly perfect God would recognise it.
The shape he wants hides in the handled wood;
he measures, gazes, plans nearly till dark
flanked by the tools hung neat on the shed wall.
The day was good.

Indoors a small boy with a wooden spoon
beats on a saucepan, trying out its music.
He wants to learn how loud a noise can get,
so bangs and sings a kind of backing tune.
The tumbler drier is humming in support.
He hasn't finished yet.

His sister's on her skate-board in the street
with arms outspread along the welcoming air,
trying to mount the runway's concrete slope.
She feels the world roll underneath her feet.
She concentrates, repeats, traps unawares
a buoyant hope.

THE BUS TO UBIDABIA

You show me from the train the stop it leaves from,
the lighted sign that gives the destination.
You're always good with buses.

Halfway along our carriage a child is singing
'Sunlight in Ubidabia' and I think,
Life is so good, I'd like to have it twice.

Then I wake and it isn't. Bombing and devastation
fill the news as I do the washing up.
Everything's rubble, the commentator says.

Several thousand people have fled their homes.
I ponder why the child in my dream was singing,
but that's absurd, since she was only me.

So where, even in sleep, could I imagine
the innocent place the child sang of might lie?
Anyway, in my dream the last bus had left.

QUASAR

Casual, she stands in the kitchen doorway,
after-image holding a saucepan.
She is nothing: this beloved ceased to exist
billions of years ago.

She has such beautiful hair,
which my reason dishevels.

She gives me light out of her emptiness.
Still her unmeaning form
keeps shining towards me, rays from the empty spaces,
bland hologram.

I watch her with my ghost of love,
its immortal remains.

She tells me to go, she whose light comes
from the person I loved in the Jurassic age
when my faith in her moved mountains,
crumpled and bent them like leaves.

What dark is now in the space she looks from,
visible, starlike, dispersed?

NIGHT SHIFT

Dark thins. A hasty choosing
behind the tender lids brings
last performances.
A final twirl for the missed-the-train gang!
One more pirouette for gone-to-work-in-pyjamas!

You hazy, vaguely threatening figures, go away –
the scene has altered.
Day is near. Instantly
whole manuscripts litter the floor, their stories
worked out in nightmare detail.

Daylight is the editor;
decisive. Glances at unsolicited offerings,
muttering, 'No... no... no.' Accepts little
into the white boardroom of morning.
Marks the rest, 'Return'.

And they'll be back
one night when the postbag is opened. Not yet. Not yet.
At the squat the partying buskers, turfed out again
with the curfew of dawn,
rehearse their material in secret.

OPENING

Beginnings
breathe out like misty plans, over the table
collecting itself for breakfast. Knife to plate:
an opening gambit.

Pausing,
the silent saucerer holds the teapot up,
choosing its square; in the magical morning hush
allocating positions.

Suddenly
murmurs from close to the ear, from the chimney breast,
like an oracular voice within the heart:
roo-coo, roo-coo,

roo –
cut off in mid-phrase like a startling thought.
The day's begun already: the spell has caught.
Each morning opens

prophetic
with such rehearsal of endings; the fallen oak
in the acorn, the deed in the idea (that's magic)
the word fruiting.

MY BUTCHER

My butcher and I, over liver and sausages,
while lunchtime radio annotates the day,
sort through strikes, unemployment, declining morals.
His hands hack and sever, neaten and tidy away.

He's all for standards, deterrents, obedience, order.
I nod and wonder, take out my purse and pay.
There's little to do but agree; his trenchant verdicts
chop through the bone of contention, leave nothing to say.

Gutted, dissected, the country's problems are finally
laid out in portions for practised hands to weigh.
There'd be little left of the one o'clock news by teatime
if they settled things swiftly and simply, my butcher's way.

LONGSTAY

Long ago I left
the smoothly-rounded, leisured southern vowels
of places to dwell in:
Stowe, Sunbury, Southwold,

and took the northern road
into a colder climate among limestone hills,
where tongues less sure of a welcome
clack sharper sounds:

plain, Danelaw place names
fit for hailing out to travellers,
sounds from rough ground –
Skegness, Scawby, Scunthorpe.

And now my tongue becomes
forgetful of the old, unhurried syllables
it still produces.
Under its roof

the words of here foregather,
harsh, back-throated, bringing
the taste of their shapes in my mouth,
describing home,

until I don't suppose
I shall go back into the soft counties
before I have become
mi luv, nanan, her across t'road.

BRAILLE

The library's steady rustle of pages
halts at the soft chuckle of a blind woman
taking the whole of a table with her great brown volumes,
her fingers enjoying a joke no one else can see.

Readers begin to handle the corners of books
here in the high room, and grainy varnish
grows into contours under the soft pads of thumbs;
chairs beneath buttocks declare their forgotten shape.

Outside a lime tree opens scaly buds,
dreaming of flowers; in the fruit shop
skins of tangerines are oily, scented,
bananas rough at the end, then smoothly inviting.

The blind woman makes for the exit, unhesitating,
thanks the assistant with a smile. Her passage downstairs
leaves us listeners sensing now, below her,
brass door-handle, steps on to pavement, breeze of the street.

LESSON

The woman stands up, stretches,
gold against the pink wall.
She's been telling me a story
concerning the Urdu for 'banana'
and the English shopkeeper
saying it one day for an Asian customer.
We laugh together,
enjoy the tangled thread of speech.
'Orright,' she says. 'Next week. Orright,'
as I push papers into the lesson folder,
fish out the car keys.

Outside I come across her mother,
cotton garments billowing round her thinness
as she takes a little sun.
I nod. She puts her hands together, comes close,
speaking by gesture and wide bony smile.
We stand, no word in common,
conversing silently where light slips past
the housing scheme's flagged entrance
and glints the silver speckles on her shoulder.
My student glances, curious, from the window.

At last she steps away
still smiling and I leave,
a little more acquainted with this language
that makes me hold my tongue,
till as I back and turn, she waves me off
like one who profited.

NAMING THE WEEDS

Sunday. I walk the garden path
where sun-blotched paving warms my feet.
This border's rich confusion shows me
weeds whose generations
are fifty years, a hundred years
older than the house, the street.
I name their blossoming:
                    violet, figwort, viper's bugloss, vetch.

Our garden logs the years
in layers of planted hopes, yet weeds endure,
old words tucked under the hem of speech,
leafing up unnoticed till a sudden colour
lights the hedge bottom and reminds me,
sends me back to the flower book to be sure
I'm naming them right:
                    enchanter's nightshade, self-heal, fox-and-cubs.

A rain shower drives me in, to move aside
leaf patterned curtains and stare out
across a garden full of words. Tansy, *etym. unknown,*
perhaps linked to the Greek for immortality,
holds up its yellow buttons. I watch seasons pass
while buried names like little bursts of thought
spring from neglected corners:
                    coltsfoot, bittercress, toadflax, poppy, spurge.

IN THE GARDEN

In the beginning
words are part of what occurs,
happen before your face
like 'thunder' when the wet air
sinks heavy into the grass, freighted with darkness,
or 'spring' touching the twigs with haze before any leaf.

A damp stone
in the beginning lies half buried in soil
and a bird fidgets beside it.
Out in the garden words are not demanded
but offer themselves,
the animals aren't yet named.

Wait here a while,
patient as the leaf buds
defining themselves gradually, starting with green.
Say nothing. Words are not yet whole
but you can listen for them –
their whisper is everywhere.

As each leaf opens
it sharpens into focus, definition:
oblong, lanceolate, rhombic –
it has decided. Next year's foliage
loiters in its nowhere. Tomorrow's idea
gathers in a wordless fluid, rises slowly.

APRIL

Outside the town the trees are thinking green.
There's nothing yet to see
unless an edge of wood
offers a longways glimpse. Stand here. No, here.
Now the view changes; now it looks like spring.

In city centres warmer air brings on
earlier growth. There knobbly buds
burst with impatient speed,
not wandering into leaf as lingeringly
as country woodland can.

Am I like town or country? Sometimes it's clear –
like yesterday, when you said,
Let's drive out to the country,
and from an indoor morning I was shaken
into a long view of the opening year.

AROMA THERAPY

Gulping the wind, herring gulls
open their pulsing throats on every roof
to drink the sea's nearness

while at ground level
in honeysuckle's comforting embrace
gardeners lean by low stone walls;
buddleia rolls them in sweetness
but in the depths of roses float
ideas like a cool voyage.

Down in the grass go snails,
their eager horns stretched after promises:
sap is good to them; the shady fig
offers its gallery of elbows. On wet nights
they go on pilgrimage up the steps,
form processions, honour their god of rain.

WILLOW

Within the city, *salix felix*
rooting in the stream
of the timber merchant's yard,
rooting and resting,

at repose in the city, in the unused corner
behind the warehouse, below the roadside wall.
No eastern weeper, but native here
under dull skies.

In the grey heart
of stony Sheffield
leaf-buds are opening, female catkins
spreading and declaring themselves,

juices rising with the same fervour
under the bark's wrinkled map
as in the deep mulch of shires.
The solitary tree shines out,

a bright particular star, to catch
the gaze and affections of passers-by,
polished with so much watching, drinking
the city stream, upholstering the road with leaves.

DAYBREAK

Each morning woken to hear
a magpie's shout a great-tit's rocking song
the pine trees repeating their seaside noise

the upstairs neighbour crossing our bedroom ceiling
scaffolders clanking poles into a lorry
clatter of glass from the bottle bin,

I gather up these fragments,
a few more pieces of the created world,
what we inherit and what we make.

I take and carry them through the day
stepping across a lattice of moments
now and now, working or resting,

and though I can't see ahead yet listening
to be aware, on watch, set
to respond, to rejoice.

HIDE

A wooden silence so dark
the floor is invisible, the shutters
defined only by blades of sunlight.
We feel our way to a bench,
steadying our feet between its uprights,
settle, pause.

When we open up
it's the fourth day of creation.
Moorhen and coot, grebe ferrying their young,
pattern the lake's glitter with black and brown
while over the teeming water mallard fly.
Dazzled, we stare

as though we had entered
a world beyond our knowledge
and come upon a different use for seeing
or as though sight itself invented
this fine embroidery of clouds and ripples,
of birds and air.

CORNELIAN CHERRY

It was early in the year, a fine March.
I was exploring the suburb
and how it opened out from streets of houses.
I was in search

of sights and wonders on the almost country road.
Suddenly from the huge garden that bordered it
fistfuls of yellow sparklers reached towards me
like party invitations.

I stopped to stare, trying to understand
the strange leafless beautiful construction,
then bore it home in my mind
to my book of trees.

The next time I went to find it, it had faded,
retracting its fingers. The time after,
had retreated, playing statues
among its fellow trees.

Now I can't find it, vanished among the thickets
of how things used to be. Perhaps next year, I think –
a time no easier to read
than the entangled past.

From the window the eye ranges
up to the green horizon
down to the bosomy garden,
its ordered sweeps of green,
cypress, laburnum, laurel.

The dense canopy holds,
surely, a thousand nests,
little empires, and every leaf
its microscopic dependents,
a population of millions.

Above the watered gardens
air is free and unmeasured.
Birds from open space
look down on perchable branches.
Freely the eye roams onward

finding more trees until
it reaches the fenced plantation
whose evergreens cap the hill
under a throw of cloud.
Farther still, out of range, the sea.

WERE THERE TRAMS IN ODESSA?
(overheard question)

Sepia. Tall house-fronts, pale above the dark streets.
Three tiny figures in heavy coats,
walking. What year is it?

It is the sepia year of long ago.
There was no time then. Streets were empty,
shops unvisited.

Inscrutable stillness, the camera's moment
fixed against the flickering human eye.
Caged in history.

No. The picture's imagined, conjured up
by that creative tool the hopeful brain
which mixes memory and invention.

But such a place and such a year existed
outside the mind's embroidery. There was trade,
there were marriages,

as in the nameless photographs which drop
out of an album from your mother's youth –

But then of course they knew if there were trams.
An easy question.

ANONYMOUS

Not where I meant to be.
I'd gone to hear the bishop talk – I forget,
on God, no doubt, and God's mysterious ways.
When I entered the room full of people
they smiled at me but I knew none of them.

The circle of chairs filled up.
The leader – let's call her Sonia – gave a welcome.
It was only then I realised where I was.
I said my name at my turn.
They waited silently for my confession.

I couldn't tell them lies or make-believe
since they were working at the truth.
I didn't speak of any struggles, failures,
or why I'd come. How could I?
I breathed into the quiet after my name.

How difficult it is, being alive.
Some told of small successes, some of none.
I merely shook my head. At the end we stood,
held hands and spoke together. Then I joined in.
Speaking is the hardest thing.

MISSING THE TURN

Told with careful exactness on the phone
how the road wound up from the village between fields,
but failing to see the sign as I drove by,
ten minutes later I came to the other end:
back among houses, a stillness of afternoon –
two women with pushchairs, a dog trailing a chain.

I turned and drove back over the motorway
among damp ploughland, found the sign, which pointed
up what had seemed a cart-track, to the big house.
So many residents, in a mulch of silence.
Led upstairs, I sat with the one I knew.

Talk wound up and down the lanes of her situation.
Now, when I think of her, why don't I see Kathleen
in her small room, speaking of doubt and grief,
but only the far end, nameless and unforeseen,
with an escaped dog nosing a playground slide?

THE WORDS

Sometimes at night, rather than ripples of sleep
come trickles of words like flow from a stuck tap –
cyan, or *alacrity, febrile, Kathmandu.* Repeated.
What are they doing, fidgeting in my skull?
They make no sense.

Or perhaps while I'm getting a meal
or putting my coat on or going down the stairs
Hesperides, lucid or maybe *integument*
will climb into my thoughts, uninvited guest
pushing in from nowhere.

Imagine the silence in the beginning, the Spirit
brooding the waters, hatching form from void.
Out of those depths of quiet worlds could grow,
the Word choosing its moment. Then Adam
busied himself with names.

If there is anywhere some herb of quiet –
chamomile, lavender, lemon balm, valerian,
wind-borne essence settling below the tongue –
let me discover it and breathe it in
and rediscover peace.

YELLOW

That shouting yellow
says *You won't be with us long,*
you'll be out of here, but we,
we're here to stay.

Forty-eight summers
since we moved in with the baby.
The bushes were smaller, the grass rougher,
but the yellow was here:

a note of defiance,
an all-out declaration, an incautious
no-going-back, unrepentant
primary colour

outstaring eyeballs
which rise to it time after time
like small fish to a fly. But look,
at the edge of the path

flotillas of yellow cups already
anticipate next week's additions
You wait, say the flowers.
You'll have gone for good but we'll be back.

PHILIPPA DANCING

There's no one else there, only the radio
and the cat comfortable between the pot plants.
No one is telling her to be careful on the stairs,
to remember her stick,
to sit down and they'll bring her a cup of tea.

The kitchen is astir with the sun that gleams into corners.
It polishes the toes of her slippers
as she jigs from table to sink, from sink to dresser,
tea towel across her shoulder
a bandolier declaring her independence.

She knows that if they were spying on her
through the corner window
they would think her reliving the dance hall nights of her youth,
but she is seizing today
in a jubilation of steps.

PARASOL

We four sat round the table talking.
Above us your parasol staved off the sun's extreme,
but all the same
a breeze let it keep up a commentary,
ruffling the canvas top
as though to say
That's what you think but there's another way.

We sketched a plan, cautiously looked ahead –
in a few weeks maybe we'd meet again.
Yet maybe then
we'd be confined to home once more
and there would be
no chance for face-to-face
even in your garden or an open space.

We'd been discussing divine and mortal knowledge.
Did bees ever forget which were their hives?
Could Jesus when a man foresee our lives?
Could we predict our children's futures, who
they would become, from their first years?
Or even hope to see
some ten years on, how sad or happy we ourselves would be?

The garden blossomed round us and the bees
toiled on, quite certain about what they did
to raise the generation which they fed.
Without their confidence, we hesitated
over our plans. How certain are the stats
which science or sociology foretell?
Lord knows said the parasol.

MOVING DAY

One, two, three
       and we vault
              across the valley and land

here in another postcode
where a squirrel fossicks in the rain
on the moss-lumpy roof of now our garage
and the back of my mind says
when we get home
but we are home.

We wake to a mild, damp day
and walls of boxes. Oddments which can't be returned
to drawers which are ours no longer.
The unencumbered squirrel sits on its haunches
and enjoys the air.

We are in the sky,
living among treetops in the region
fir cones drop from. Out of the window
we sense the passing traffic of radio waves.

The future crouching in the valley
opens its arms as the sun rises and the row of pines
retract their shadows and whisper of possibilities.
We empty and stow, fight through our box walls like prisoners
digging a way out. Evening comes.

Morning comes, the fourth day. Birds look in at us
from their neighbourly branches. We are here
for keeps. Day passes. Far down the valley
an owl couches his soft notes on silence.

ACKNOWLEDGEMENTS

Thanks are due to the editors of the following publications in which some of these poems have previously appeared:
Artemis, Envoi, The Ground Beneath her Feet (Cinnamon Press 2008), *Iron, New Poetry 3 (*Arts Council, 1977*), New Poetry 8* (Arts Council / Hutchinson, 1982), *New Poetries VIII* (Carcanet, 2021), *The New Review, Orbis, Other Poetry, PN Review, Pennine Platform, Poems of Peace and War* (Oxford 1979*), The Result is What you See Today* (Smith|Doorstop, 2019), *The Rialto, Seam, The Sheffield Anthology* (Smith|Doorstop, 2012), *Smiths Knoll, Spinning a Yarn – Weaving a Poem* (A Sheffield Community Heritage Project, 2018), *Stand, Staple, The Tablet, TLS.*

A number have also been published in one of my three pamphlets, *Letting the Dark Through* (Mandeville 1981) and from Smith|Doorstop, *Tenants,* 2014 and *Midsummer,* 2020.

'In the House' won third prize in the Yorkshire Open Poetry Competition in 1993.

'Missing the Turn' won the Norwich Poetry Society Competition in 1994.

'Braille' won second prize in the Bridport Prize Competition in 2003.

'Milk' was broadcast on BBC Radio 4 in November 1983

'Were there Trams in Odessa?' was broadcast as 'poem of the week' on BBC Radio 3 in June 2020.

My particular thanks are due both to The Arvon Foundation and The Poetry Business for inspiration and encouragement, to Peter Scupham and to Ann and Peter Sansom for editorial help with the three pamphlets and to Michael Schmidt and all the team at Carcanet for making this book possible. Also to my various poetry friends, especially the three made at Lumb Bank (Meg Cox, Marilyn Francis, Pru Kitching) for much careful reading and for friendship. And above all to Edmund for shrewd judgements and unfailing support.

THIS
BOOK
WAS SET IN
CASLON LETTERING
WITH GILL SANS NOVA
TITLING BY
CARCANET